PETER LOURIE

ON THE TEXAS TRAIL
OF
CABEZA DE VACA

BOYDS MILLS PRESS

HONESDALE, PENNSYLVANIA

Text and photographs © 2008 by Peter Lourie
All rights reserved
Designed by Tim Gillner

Boyds Mills Press, Inc.
815 Church Street
Honesdale, Pennsylvania 18431
Printed in China

Library of Congress Cataloging-in-Publication Data

Lourie, Peter.
 On the Texas trail of Cabeza de Vaca / Peter Lourie. — 1st ed.
   p. cm.
 ISBN 978-1-59078-492-1 (hardcover : alk. paper)
 1. Núñez Cabeza de Vaca, Alvar, 16th cent.—Travel—Texas—Juvenile literature. 2. Explorers—America—Biography—Juvenile literature.
3. Explorers—Texas—Biography—Juvenile literature. 4. Explorers—Spain—Biography—Juvenile literature. 5. Texas—Description and
travel—Juvenile literature. 6. Texas—History—To 1846—Juvenile literature. 7. Texas—Discovery and exploration—Spanish—Juvenile
literature. 8. America—Discovery and exploration—Spanish—Juvenile literature. I. Title.
 E125.N9L65 2008
 976.4'01—dc22

                    2007049180

First edition
The text of this book is set in 12-point Berkeley Book.

10 9 8 7 6 5 4 3 2 1

Excerpts from *The Journey of Álvar Núñez Cabeza de Vaca, Translated from His Own Narrative* by Fanny Bandelier. New York: A. S. Barnes, 1905.

Excerpt on page 13 from *The Narrative of Cabeza de Vaca* by Álvar Núñez Cabeza de Vaca, edited, translated, and with an introduction by Rolena Adorno and Patrick Charles Pautz. Lincoln: University of Nebraska Press, 2003.

Additional Photographs

Back jacket:
Peter Lourie (tree)
Donald Olson (pine nuts)
Florida State Archives (stamp)
Texas State University–San Marcos, Wittliff Collections, Southwestern Writers Collection (book)
University of South Florida, Tampa Campus Library (map)

Jacket and interior: Vintage paper © Stephen Mulcahey: image from bigstockphoto.com

Blocker History of Medicine Collections, Moody Medical Library, The University of Texas Medical Branch, Galveston, Texas, USA: 30, *The First Recorded Surgical Operation in North America: Cabeza de Vaca, 1535*, copyright © 1965 by Tom Lea

Florida State Archives: Jacket image of Cabeza de Vaca

Frederic Remington Art Museum: 27, *Cabeza de Vaca in the Desert* by Frederic Remington, 1905. Frederic Remington Art Museum, Ogdensburg, New York

Grabhorn Press: 40, signature from *La Relación* by Cabeza de Vaca. San Francisco: Grabhorn Press, 1929

Library of Congress: 10 (top and bottom), from *The Life, Travels, and Adventures of Ferdinand de Soto, Discoverer of the Mississippi* by Lambert A. Wilmer. Philadelphia: J. T. Lloyd, 1858, p. 307, John William Orr (1815–1887), engraver; 13 (top), Charles V, 1902, etched by Jacques Reich (1852–1923), from an engraving by Iovita Guravaglia and after the portrait by Niccola Bettoni; 43, *Coronado's March–Colorado* by Frederic Remington, 1897; 44; 45

Donald Olson: 16, from *Texas History Stories #1* by E. G. Littlejohn. Richmond: B. F. Johnson Publishing Company, 1901; 34; 35 (top left); 36 (bottom), map from "The First Europeans in Texas, 1528–1536" by Harbert Davenport and Joseph K. Wells, *Southwestern Historical Quarterly*, vol. 22, 1918–1919

Rosenberg Library, Galveston, Texas: 17, map, *Plan du Port decouvert dans le Golfe du Mexique le 21. d'Aoust 1721* par mr. Bénard de la Harpe (1725) [Map of port discovered in the Gulf of Mexico, 21 August 1721, by Bénard de la Harpe]

Texas State University–San Marcos, Southwestern Writers Collection, Wittliff Collections: 13 (bottom), 1555 edition of Cabeza de Vaca's *La relación y comentarios*

University of South Florida, Tampa Campus Library, Special Collections Department: 12, map, *La Florida*, 1584

Acknowledgments

I could not have followed the Texas trail of Cabeza de Vaca without the help of the following people. First and foremost, I want to heartily thank Donald Chipman, Ph.D., professor emeritus of history, the University of North Texas at Denton. All through this project, Dr. Chipman offered invaluable advice. His books on the colonial Southwest and his many articles about the route of Cabeza de Vaca were the backbone of my own musings. Equally helpful were Donald W. Olson, Ph.D., Department of Physics, and his wife, Marilynn S. Olson, Ph.D., Department of English, Texas State University at San Marcos. They encouraged me to visit El Chilpitin canyon and for many hours allowed me to pore over their maps of the Monclova area. Don Olson's article on the pine nuts is one of the most interesting bits of research I have ever read. Also, I could not have written this book without the help of David La Vere, Ph.D., Department of History, the University of North Carolina Wilmington. Never have I met a scholar with such generosity of spirit. His insight into the real meaning of Cabeza de Vaca's enslavement by the natives of the Galveston area was most helpful.

In addition, I would like to thank Steve Davis, assistant curator, and Joel Minor, processing archivist, at the Southwestern Writers Collection, Texas State University at San Marcos, who allowed me to view the 1555 edition of Cabeza de Vaca's *La Relación*; Mary Hernandez, archival assistant, Rosenberg Library, Galveston, Texas, who supplied me with a wonderful old map of Galveston Bay; and Juan Manuel Zambrano Gonzalez, who helped me find El Chilpitin canyon and did so with good humor and a spirit of adventure.

—P.L.

Chaque

Lacane

Aijx

Xualatino

Vlibahalj

Quigata

Tasralifa

Achusj

R. de S. Spirito

R. de Coniauerat

R. de Flores

R. de Nines

R. de Veruos

R. de piscatores

R. de Gigantes

R. de Loro

C. desierto

C. de Cruz

P. Hondo

Rio Escondido

Terra Baxca

Mar
pequeno

Cacos

Culias

Medanos de
la Magdale.

R. de Palmas

R. S. Paulo.

TROPICVS CANCRI.

Lago de
salinas

Y. de Alacranes

Y. de Arenas

Tamos

Y. de Negras

CONTENTS

Texas

Rio Grande

Galveston

Gulf
of
Mexico

Mexico

Mexico City

Pacific
Ocean

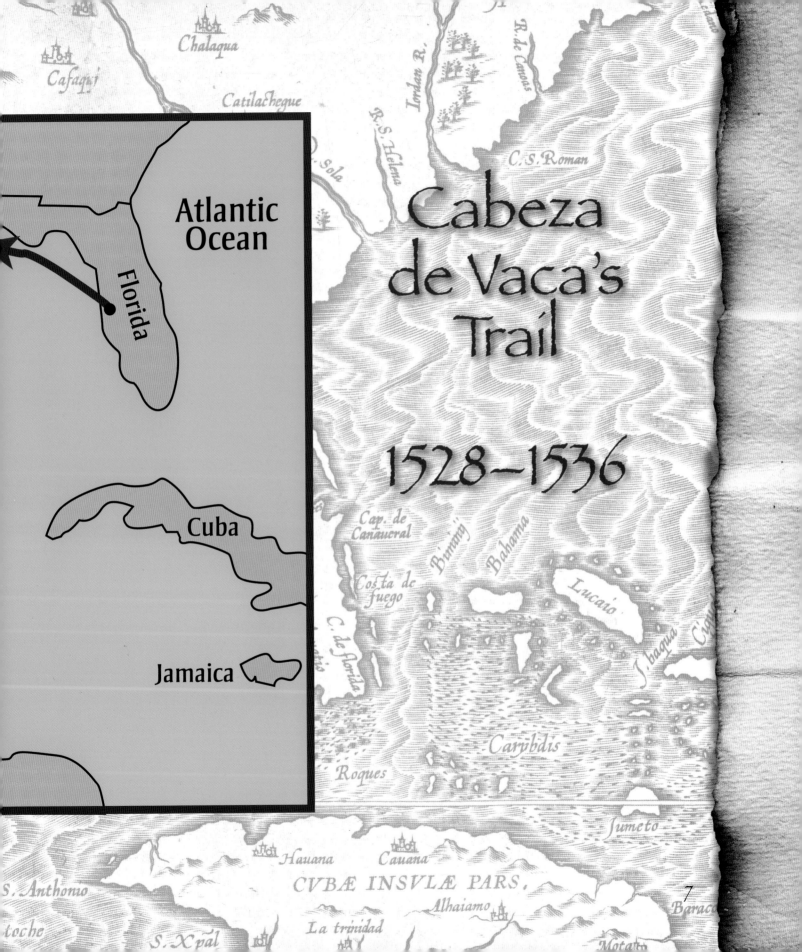

Chalaqua

Cafaqui

Catilacheque

Jordan R.

R. de Canoes

R. S. Helena

Sola

C. S. Roman

Atlantic Ocean

Florida

Cuba

Jamaica

Cabeza de Vaca's Trail

1528–1536

Cap. de Canaueral

Costa de fuego

C. de florida

Roques

Bimini

Bahama

Lucaio

J. baqua

Carybdis

Jumeto

S. Anthonio

Hauana

Cauana

CVBÆ INSVLÆ PARS.

Alhaiamo

La trinidad

S. Xpal

toche

Baraco

Mota

On the 27th day of the month of June, 1527, the Governor Pánfilo de Narváez departed from the port of San Lucar de Barrameda, with authority and orders from Your Majesty to conquer and govern the provinces that extend from the river of the Palms to the Cape of Florida . . . The fleet he took along consisted of five vessels, in which went about 600 men. The officials he had with him (since they must be mentioned) were those here named: Cabeza de Vaca, treasurer and alguacil mayor [sheriff]; Alonso Enríquez, purser; Alonso de Solis, factor of Your Majesty and inspector. A friar of the order of Saint Francis, called Fray Juan, went as commissary, with four other monks of the order.

—Cabeza de Vaca

Searching for the Trail

Sixteenth-century Spanish conquerors, known as conquistadors, came to the New World with a violent thirst for gold and land. When the conquistadors returned to Spain, they told fantastic stories about their adventures.

One story stands out from the rest, about a conquistador whose expedition was a complete failure. Cabeza de Vaca collected no gold and conquered no one, but he accomplished a feat no other conquistador had. After spending years among the native peoples of the New World, he learned to respect the very people he had come to conquer.

In 1527 Álvar Núñez Cabeza de Vaca set sail for *La Florida* from Spain under the command of Pánfilo de Narváez. The goal of the expedition was to explore and colonize a large, unknown area extending from the present-day state of Florida to Mexico, north of Tampico. After landing near Tampa Bay in 1528, Narváez split his forces and traveled inland. The journey northward was a disaster. Narváez's men ran out of food and were attacked by Indians.

Conquistadors bound for the New World set sail from Spanish ports, often with great fanfare.

Finally, when Narváez's ships failed to return for him and his men, 258 soldiers built five crude rafts from horsehides and trees, hoping to reach Mexico. Beset by storms, thirst, and starvation, they worked their way west along the Gulf Coast, past the Mississippi River, to the present-day Galveston, Texas, area. Narváez perished when his raft was blown out to sea. His second-in-command, Cabeza de Vaca, landed somewhere on or near Galveston Island and spent the next six years with various native tribes.

Out of the 258 men who came ashore at La Florida, only four would survive—Cabeza de Vaca himself, along with Alonso del Castillo Maldonado, Andrés Dorantes de Carranca, and Esteban, a Moroccan-born slave. In 1534 these four survivors fled their native captors and trudged many hundreds of miles to Mexico City, the city that Hernán Cortés had taken from the Aztecs only a few years before.

The exact route the four survivors took is debated. Some say they took the "northern route," also known as the "trans-Texas route," across west Texas, New Mexico, and Arizona. More likely, the castaways took the "southern route" and followed the coast south into Mexico, then across the Mexican desert.

Cabeza de Vaca returned to Spain to write an account of his discoveries in the New World. Published in 1542 for the king of Spain, *La Relación*, or *The Account*, is unique among the writings of the Spanish conquest. Unlike other conquest narratives, *La Relación* presents a sympathetic picture of the people Cabeza de Vaca encountered. He never considers himself superior to them as most conquistadors had.

Álvar Núñez Cabeza de Vaca, having survived shipwrecks, hurricanes, starvation, and Indian attacks, became the first European ever to cross the North American continent, the first to describe the people who lived there, the first to write about the flora and fauna he encountered, the first to see the possum and the buffalo, the first to see the Mississippi River, and the first nonnative Texan. He and his three companion survivors were like the *Star Trek* crew on the spaceship *Enterprise*, going out into space,

Many in the Narváez expedition met a terrible fate, as depicted in a nineteenth-century engraving.

exploring new galaxies and a world that had not yet been seen by others. Only decades after Christopher Columbus's daring expedition to the New World, Cabeza de Vaca's journey was a further exploration into the unknown.

Cabeza de Vaca also paved the way for other explorers, such as Francisco Vásquez de Coronado, who explored the Southwest, and Hernando de Soto, who set off in search of the Pacific Ocean based on what he had heard firsthand from Cabeza de Vaca.

Nearly five hundred years after Cabeza de Vaca, I headed out for the Lone Star State to follow in the conquistador's footsteps, or at least to travel in the vicinity of his route, since no one knows for sure where he passed. Cabeza de Vaca had survived among the native people of Texas for almost seven years of his eight-year ordeal. The man I most wanted to meet before I began my trek was Donald Chipman.

Dr. Chipman of Denton, Texas, a retired professor of history, has researched Cabeza de Vaca extensively. In 2003 Dr. Chipman was honored by the king of Spain for his work on the colonial Southwest.

On a map, Dr. Chipman showed me the route I could take along the coast, including the back roads that would best approximate the travels of Cabeza de Vaca through Texas.

Historians study original documents or sources, often called primary sources. They also review secondary sources, such as books and articles written about those primary sources. Then they bring in other disciplines, such as the study of geography and animals and plants. Dr. Chipman had carefully studied all of this material in his research on Cabeza de Vaca.

Though no one can know for certain where Cabeza de Vaca traveled in Texas, his account of his adventure offers clues. Dr. Chipman told me that with a close reading of the *Relación*, "You can pretty well identify where Cabeza was and where he went when he left the Indians for the last time. What I've done is to help establish that it was the coastal route, the southern route, that these guys took and not the trans-Texas route. The northern-route idea ignores Cabeza's description of the flora and fauna and the actual land forms and the rivers."

When I asked Chipman if he himself had ever tried to find the areas where Cabeza de Vaca might have spent those six years around Galveston, he looked at me as if I were a little bit crazy and said, "Heck no. What are you going to see in a city like Houston—nothing but traffic and freeways and congestion. On the coast it's all high-rises. What's left of the land Cabeza de Vaca saw? Not much."

Donald Chipman points to the symbol of the Texas Surgical Society, the head of a cow imposed on the Star of Texas. It commemorates the first surgery in Texas, performed by Cabeza de Vaca, whose name means "head of a cow."

Conquistadors

Conquistadors (meaning "conquerors") were Spanish soldiers, explorers, and adventurers who led the Spanish conquest of Mexico and Peru in the sixteenth century, starting with Christopher Columbus and his 1492 settlement in what is now the Dominican Republic and Haiti. He was followed by Hernán Cortés, who conquered the Aztecs in Mexico in 1521. Francisco Pizarro and Hernando de Soto went on to conquer the Incan Empire of Peru in 1532.

Sometimes it is easy to glorify the deeds of the past and those who accomplished them, but the Spanish conquistadors were ruthless men on a ruthless mission: to conquer the New World and hunt for gold. In their quest, they killed native peoples and destroyed civilizations. In this regard, Cabeza de Vaca was unlike other conquistadors.

In A Short Account of the Destruction of the Indies (1552), a Dominican monk named Bartolomé de Las Casas recorded detailed descriptions of the cultures he encountered in the Caribbean, Central America, and what is now Mexico. He also described the ugly side of the conquest, the actions of the conquistadors themselves. He wrote how the Spaniards cruelly murdered the native peoples. With their spears and horses, the Spaniards spared no one, not the old men, not the old women, not even the children. They "cut them to pieces as if slaughtering lambs in a field."

When Chipman pointed to the various back roads on the map that might approximate Cabeza de Vaca's route south, however, he looked interested and said I might indeed find landscapes similar to the way it was more than 470 years ago. "Certainly wilder terrain than Houston," he said with a smile.

La Relación

I traveled first to the Texas State University library at San Marcos. An archivist in the Southwestern Writers Collection brought out the library's prize possession, the rare 450-year-old edition of Cabeza de Vaca's *La Relación*. The book was in remarkably good shape. I turned the thick pages with protective white gloves that the library requires researchers to wear. The print was dark and clear.

Cabeza de Vaca's book had been his special gift to Charles V—not the customary offering of riches, land, and mineral wealth from a conquistador. Rather, it was the gift of information, descriptions of the uncharted lands and unknown peoples of New Spain. In the time of Cabeza de Vaca, New Spain included the Caribbean islands, the land that stretched from present-day Florida to Baja California, and Mexico.

The Spanish territory that Ponce de León named La Florida, as shown in this map created in 1584, almost fifty years after Cabeza de Vaca's journey.

Cabeza de Vaca writes:

I had no opportunity to perform greater service than this, which is to bring to Your Majesty an account of all that I was able to observe and learn in the nine years that I walked lost and naked through many and very strange lands. [With no means of accurately measuring time, Cabeza de Vaca miscalculated how long he wandered through the New World. It was slightly less than eight years.]

Half of the *Relación* records Cabeza de Vaca's experiences in what is now Texas. During these six and a half "Texas" years, Cabeza de Vaca learned to communicate in many native languages and came to know the customs of peoples never described until then and, by the way, not encountered again until the French explorer René Robert Cavelier, Sieur de La Salle, traveled to the region more than 150 years later.

Charles V, for whom Cabeza de Vaca wrote La Relación. *During Charles's reign, Spain conquered Mexico and Peru.*

Holding the treasured 1555 edition of La Relación *was a thrilling moment.*

The title page of the 1555 edition of Cabeza de Vaca's La relación y comentarios, *often known in English as* The Account.

Close to shore a wave took us and hurled the barge a horse's length out of the water. With the violent shock nearly all the people who lay in the boat like dead came to themselves, and, seeing we were close to land, began to crawl out on all fours. As they took to some rocks, we built a fire and toasted some of our maize. We found rain water, and with the warmth of the fire people revived and began to cheer up.

—*Cabeza de Vaca*

Getting to Know
Cabeza de Vaca

It was a rough landing near present-day
Galveston, Texas, on November 6, 1528. Having sailed west for six
weeks along the Gulf Coast in a vain search for Spanish settlements,
only two of five rafts remained. The disappearance of expedition
leader Narváez, along with everyone on his raft, left Cabeza de Vaca
in charge of those who survived. With little water and food, eighty
weakened and near-dead Spaniards tumbled onto the shore of a
small island in the middle of what seemed like nowhere.

The men explored the island and came across deserted campsites.
One man stole a dog and some supplies. Suddenly a hundred
Karankawa Indians with bows drawn appeared out of the brush. Cabeza
de Vaca communicated with them, and they exchanged bells and beads
for arrows, a sign of friendship. The Indians came back over the next
several days with fish and roots to feed the weakened Spaniards.

Strengthened, the castaways attempted to launch the damaged
raft, but the waves drove them back onto the beach. A few died in
the attempt. Those who lived had shed all their clothes. For weeks
now they hadn't eaten anything except toasted maize.

Cabeza de Vaca writes:

The rest of us, as naked as we had been born, had lost everything. ... It was in November, bitterly cold, and we in such a state that every bone could easily be counted, and we looked like death itself.

The Karankawas were horrified at the sight of the destitute Spaniards, three of whom lay dead on the beach. They began to cry in a loud, ceremonial weeping, which made the Spaniards feel even worse.

Cabeza de Vaca asked the Karankawas to take them to their village. The Spaniards were picked up and carried "so rapidly that they almost did not let our feet touch the ground." It was a long journey. The Indians built bonfires along the route to warm the Spaniards and revive them before moving on.

When they reached the village, situated somewhere in what is now south Texas, the Karankawas put on a great celebration, dancing throughout the night. But there was little joy in it for the Spaniards, who feared they would be sacrificed. As the Indians continued to feed and care for them, however, the Spaniards began to trust their rescuers. Cabeza de Vaca noticed one of the Karankawas wearing a familiar trinket. The Indian explained that it was given to him by other Spaniards camped nearby. These turned out to be Andrés Dorantes and Alonso del Castillo, two of the four men who would be the only survivors of the ordeal.

After the Spaniards had regained their strength, five of the men, who were good swimmers, were sent down the coast in a desperate attempt to find the Spanish settlement of Pánuco, founded by Cortés in 1526 and now the city of Tampico, on the northeast coast of Mexico. At this time in the exploration of the

THE NEXT MOMENT ANOTHER WAVE COMPLETELY UPSET HER

THEN TAKING THE SPANIARDS IN THEIR ARMS, THEY CARRIED THEM TO THE NEAREST VILLAGE

An early twentieth-century illustration shows the Spaniards crashing on the shores of Galveston and their rescue by the Karankawas.

New World, there were no accurate maps of the region, and so it was impossible for Cabeza de Vaca to know how far he and his men were from Pánuco. They thought they were much closer than they actually were. The weather was cold, the food scarce. The swimmers were doomed, some reduced to cannibalism.

... [the swimmers] were driven to such an extremity that they ate each other up until but one remained, who being left alone, there was nobody to eat him. ... After a very short time, out of eighty men who had come there in our two parties only fifteen remained alive.

Wretched Island

For decades scholars have debated just where Cabeza de Vaca landed on November 6, 1528. He could have landed anywhere on the twenty-seven miles of Galveston Island beach. Some say it was west Galveston Island; others say it was farther down the coast. We will probably never know for sure. But it's safe to say that it was in the Galveston area. Wherever he landed, Cabeza de Vaca called it *Isla de Malhado*, or Island of Ill Fate. He chose the name because after one more attempt to leave, the raft sank and the men were forced to spend the winter on the island.

When I drove into Galveston, it didn't look like the Island of Ill Fate. The temperature was a perfect sixty-nine degrees on a blue-sky, sun-smeared day in March. But Chipman was right. The island is now developed with high-rises, hotels, and restaurants.

I decided to drive down the coast along the beach until the houses almost disappeared. I walked out

Galveston

Galveston Island sits 50 miles southeast of Houston, 345 miles west of the Mississippi River, and 280 miles from the Rio Grande. The island is made entirely of sand. Someone once drilled 1,500 feet down through that sand and never found underlying bedrock.

The island acts as a barrier, protecting the mainland from storms. In fact, the islands along the coast of Texas are called the Barrier Islands.

On the Galveston Bay side of the island, salt marshes and tidal flats are home to thousands of birds, alligators, and rattlesnakes. Cabeza de Vaca and the other survivors of the raft journey would have explored much of Galveston Bay, which is 17 miles wide and only 7 feet deep.

By the end of the seventeenth century, Spain was declining as a world power, and France, one of its rivals, began to explore the Gulf Coast. The first French ship sailed into Galveston Bay in 1719. This map of the bay, based on the findings of the French explorer Jean Baptiste Bénard de la Harpe, was created in 1725, almost two hundred years after Cabeza de Vaca's landing.

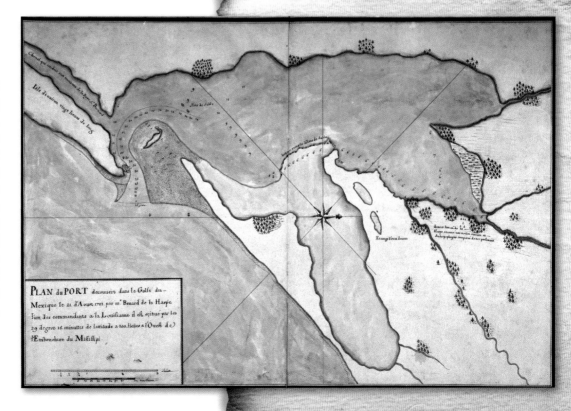

PLAN du PORT decouvert dans le Golfe du Mexique le 21 d'Aoust 1721 par mr Benard de la Harpe l'un des commandants a la Louisianne il est scitué par les 29 degrez 16 minuttes de latitude a 100 lieües a l'Ouest de l'Embouchure du Mississipi

onto the sand, looked at the water stretching to the horizon, and imagined that this was what the world may have looked like in Cabeza de Vaca's time, nearly half a millennium ago.

I found a historical marker in the weeds. As gulls circled overhead, I read on the plaque that the area had been visited by the French explorer La Salle in 1685. In 1815 it was home to the buccaneer Jean Lafitte. In the 1820s this beach was also a debarkation point for illegal slave ships.

Food sources abound in Galveston Bay: green cattails, which can be eaten like corn on the cob, and their roots, which can be crushed for flour; quahog clams; scallops; crabs; flounder; and ducks. This is plenty of food if you have the strength and knowledge to collect it—which the Spaniards did not.

Different bands of Indians took custody of Cabeza de Vaca and the fourteen other survivors. Cabeza de Vaca was sick and could not accompany his friends who traveled down the coast. He was forced to live with the Karankawas for another year.

After the initial kindnesses shown to him, Cabeza de Vaca writes, he was badly treated and forced to dig roots until his hands bled. Meanwhile, he noticed that some of the other Spanish survivors who had been taken away by other bands of Indians were already leading better lives. His account describes the people on Malhado:

> ... they have no other weapons than bows and arrows with which they are most dexterous.
> ... The women do the hard work. People stay on this island from October till the end of February, feeding on the roots I have mentioned, taken from under the water in November and December.

Cabeza de Vaca's information about the native peoples of south Texas is invaluable. For example, he records how the Karankawas treated their children. He says that they love their children more than anything or anyone and that, when one dies, they cry for that child every day for a year.

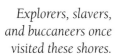

Explorers, slavers, and buccaneers once visited these shores.

Somewhere out there, Cabeza de Vaca and his companions landed on the "Island of Ill Fate."

Cabeza de Vaca the Slave?

In preparation for my journey over Cabeza de Vaca's trail, I had flown to North Carolina to meet David La Vere, a professor at the University of North Carolina Wilmington. A sturdy man with a Louisiana accent, David was friendly and helpful. He gave me his perspective on Cabeza de Vaca's view of himself as a slave.

"Was de Vaca really a slave?" I asked.

"The slavery stuff is pretty interesting," La Vere said. "First of all, slavery and the taking of captives was common, but in this case, remember, the Spaniards weren't taken as captives. They were washed ashore.

"The Europeans had a sense of entitlement, too," La Vere continued. "They came ashore in the land of the Karankawa and, immediately, they expected to be fed. So they were fed and taken care of and warmed and comforted. Even so, the Spaniards did nothing. So I think what happened after a while is they became like bad house guests.

"Finally, someone says, 'Go out there and dig that root.' They talk about abuse, but digging roots was no more abuse than what an Indian woman did. If it's abuse for a European, then why isn't it abuse for an Indian woman to dig roots and haul water?

David La Vere, an expert on the native people of south Texas.

"The Spaniards just sit around and do nothing. They don't hunt, they don't go to war, and they don't go out and get supplies. They don't have much interaction with the Indians other than demanding food.

"Eventually, the Karankawa grow tired of this and they start ordering de Vaca around. Instead of standing up for himself and saying no or fighting back, he allows himself to be slapped around. Hey, if you're going to act like a slave, well, then you *are* a slave.

"At this point, the Spaniards allow themselves to be more or less browbeaten. If you say, 'I don't dig. I don't do work. Indians dig roots, not me,' then you're going to be forced or intimidated into doing it."

At some point, though, La Vere said, Cabeza de Vaca must have changed this dynamic and gained some power. "You have to understand the concept among Indian people of personal power. Personal power is a kind of medicine, a great medicine—once a slave, not always a slave. At some point Cabeza de Vaca did something that showed he wasn't a slave. Showing more personal power allowed him to become a trader between the Karankawan and the Caddoan people to the north."

Fishing boats and bait stands line the coastal area where Cabeza de Vaca turned inland to make his escape.

Cabeza de Vaca the Trader

So where would he have traded? Perhaps along any one of the rivers in that area that runs into the Gulf of Mexico: the Trinity, the San Jacinto, the Brazos, and the Colorado. He might have traveled hundreds of miles up these rivers during the next five "Texas" years, passing by present-day Houston many times. We have absolutely no idea where he went because he does not tell us in his account. In fact, the Spanish had only a vague idea of the region's geography. Not until many expeditions later did Spain really know the size and extent of the continent or of the region called La Florida.

Inland, Cabeza de Vaca had more freedom to roam. He collected goods the coastal Indians could use. Perhaps even more importantly, he became useful, or, as La Vere suggests, he gained personal power.

This is why I went to work and joined the other Indians. Among these I improved my condition a little by becoming a trader, doing the best in it I could, and they gave me food and treated me well. They entreated me to go about from one part to another to get the things they needed, as on account of constant warfare there is neither travel nor barter in the land. So, trading along with my wares I penetrated inland as far as I cared to go and along the coast as much as forty or fifty leagues. [A league is about 3.5 miles, or the distance a person can walk in an hour.] *My stock consisted mainly of pieces of seashells and cockles, and shells with which they cut a fruit which is like a bean, used by them for healing and in their dances and feasts. This is of greatest value among them, besides shell-beads and other objects. These things I carried inland, and in exchange brought back hides and red ochre with which they rub and dye their faces and hair, flint for arrow points, glue and hard canes where-with to make them, and tassels made of the hair of deer, which they dye red. This trade suited me well because it gave me liberty to go wherever I pleased; I was not bound to do anything and no longer a slave. Wherever I went they treated me well, and gave me to eat for the sake of my wares.*

Cabeza de Vaca became well known as a trader. La Vere had cautioned me not to think of this "trading" as something we do today, not like going into a store and paying a certain price for a certain item. Trade, he said, meant haggling, and barter was difficult, because it could arouse anger. Yet Cabeza de Vaca survived. All the while he was trading, he was plotting his escape. He writes, "My principal object in doing it [trading], however, was to find out in what manner I might get further away."

While on our way it began to rain and rained the whole day. We lost the trail and found ourselves in a big forest, where we gathered plenty of leaves of prickly pears which we roasted that same night in an oven made by ourselves, and so much heat did we give them that in the morning they were fit to be eaten. After eating them we recommended ourselves to God again, and left, and struck the trail we had lost.

—Cabeza de Vaca

THREE

Farther into Texas

I drove down the coast of Texas and headed for the area Cabeza de Vaca called the "River of Nuts"—the Guadalupe River. In 1533 Cabeza de Vaca was living with the Mariames Indians, who spent a part of their year on the Guadalupe in a stretch of large pecan groves.

Driving Cabeza de Vaca's route through such swampy and gnarled coastal vegetation, I had a difficult time imagining how he survived here. He writes about the Indians making fires to keep the mosquitoes at bay. Even today the area is filled with voracious mosquitoes for most of the year. I wondered if smoke would have offered enough protection.

At the town of Brazoria, I crossed the Brazos River, mentioned in the *Relación* and certainly one of Texas's great rivers. Soon I came to the River of Nuts.

I followed Cabeza de Vaca's trail across the Brazos River.

Today small farms line the Guadalupe. When I was there in the spring, a light green spray of buds filled the trees overhanging the quiet river. The delta of the Guadalupe is an important region in Cabeza de Vaca's story. He had been separated from Dorantes and Castillo since they had gone off with various Indians in the spring of 1529, four years before. And now, with his own band of Indians in the pecan groves, he heard that three other survivors from the rafts were there, too, collecting pecans with their native captors.

> *... the Indians who kept Alonso del Castillo and Andrés Dorantes came to the very spot we had been told of to eat the nuts upon which they subsist for two months in the year, grinding certain small grains with them, without eating anything else. Even of that they do not always have, since one year there may be some and the next year not.*

In the pecan groves, Cabeza de Vaca stole off to meet his comrades. They were overjoyed. Each thought the other dead. Here on the Guadalupe River, far from Galveston Bay, they planned their escape.

I told him my purpose was to go to a country of Christians and that I followed this direction and trail. Andrés Dorantes said that for many days he had been urging Castillo and Estevanico [Esteban] to go further on, but they did not risk it, being unable to swim and afraid of the rivers and inlets that had to be crossed so often in that country. Still, as it pleased God, Our Lord, to spare me after all my sufferings and sickness and finally let me rejoin them, they at last determined upon fleeing, as I would take them safely across the rivers and bays we might meet.

When the rivers of Texas approach the Gulf of Mexico, they turn into estuaries, inland lakes, and deltas. The delta of the Guadalupe is the best example of a natural river-delta habitat in all of Texas, and it's less altered by humans than any other major river floodplain in the state. A delta is formed where rivers approach the sea, and the water slows. The flat coastal land allows sediments to settle from the water. As sediments fill channels, the river slowly meanders across a wide area. Old river channels and minor tributaries create a web of waterways, ponds, and wetlands. Here in the delta of the Guadalupe, crab, shrimp, and birds are plentiful. Cabeza de Vaca and his men would have found an abundance of turtles, catfish, garfish, alligators, crawfish, frogs, mullets, ducks, and ibis. Living with the Indians, the men finally learned how to hunt and fish.

Esteban

Esteban (sometimes spelled Estevan) was the first African American in Texas. A Muslim and a speaker of Arabic, Esteban was born in Morocco in North Africa, where later he was captured by the Spaniards. He was the slave of Captain Andrés Dorantes, another of the four survivors. Eventually, Esteban became Catholic, perhaps to find favor with his captors. He also learned to speak Spanish.

He participated with Cabeza de Vaca and the other two survivors in healing ceremonies and acted as a scout on the long journey to Mexico City. Most importantly, his skill at languages may have been a key factor in the group's ability to communicate with the many native groups they encountered as they made their way across the wide expanse of what is present-day Mexico. Without doubt, Esteban worked more as a partner than a slave during the long ordeal.

After reaching Mexico City, Esteban stayed in the New World. He guided a 1539 expedition north into what is now New Mexico in search of the fabled Seven Cities of Gold (see page 43). Esteban ranged well ahead of the expedition with a group of native people. When he came into the land of the Zuni, he was killed and the party turned back. But Francisco Vásquez de Coronado would soon follow into this same area, leading an expedition that would have among it more African slaves who had been brought to Mexico.

Land of the Prickly-Pear Cactus

Native people ate the fruit of the prickly-pear cactus. Cabeza de Vaca and his companions survived on it.

In 1533 the four survivors plotted their escape, but it would be another eighteen months before they could put their plan into action. Just as they were about to flee, a fight broke out among the Indians, and Cabeza de Vaca and his friends were hustled away by their captors. So the desperate men had to put off their plan until the following year when all the Indian bands would come together again in the land of the prickly pear.

> *... it was necessary to remain with them* [his Indian captors] *for six months longer* [from April to September 1533], *after which time they would remove to another section in order to eat prickly pears. These are a fruit of the size of eggs, red and black, and taste very good. For three months they subsist upon them exclusively, eating nothing else.*

Variously identified as Coahuiltecans, Karankawas, or Tonkawas, these people were hunters and gatherers. They drank prickly-pear juice, dried the cactus leaves for food, and pounded them into powder for cooking. The plant, whose fruit is called by the Taíno Indian word *tuna,* was readily available, and in this semidesert, people found food where they could.

All the while, Cabeza de Vaca waited for another opportunity to escape.

> *I told my companions that I would wait for them at the tunas until full moon. It was the first of September and the first day of the new moon, and I told them that if at the time set they did not appear I would go on alone without them. We parted, each one going off with his Indians.*

26

At last, they made their move. The men set out for Mexico City, first by traveling inland, away from the southern coast of Texas, on account of rumors of dangerous Indians in that region.

These Indians told us that further on there were others called Cajoles, who live nearer the coast, and that they were those who killed all the people that came [on one of the rafts]. ... They had been so emaciated and feeble that when being killed they offered no resistance. So the Indians finished with all of them, and showed us some of their clothes and weapons and said the barge was still there stranded. This is the fifth of the missing ones. That of the Governor [Pánfilo de Narváez] we already said had been swept out into the sea.

Cabeza de Vaca's turn inland around Alice, Texas, west of today's Corpus Christi, was only the beginning of the escape. Once again the men were forced to spend another eight months with yet another group of friendly Indians called the Avavares. And once again, they barely survived off prickly pear in a harsh desert environment.

Cabeza de Vaca, the figure seated in the middle, as depicted by Frederic Remington in his painting Cabeza de Vaca the Desert, *1905.*

The way we treated the sick was to make over them the sign of the cross while breathing on them, recite a Paternoster and Ave Maria, and pray to God, Our Lord, as best we could to give them good health and inspire them to do us some favors. Thanks to His will and the mercy He had upon us, all those for whom we prayed, as soon as we crossed them, told the others that they were cured and felt well again.

—*Cabeza de Vaca*

FOUR

A Mystical Turn

I drove southwest on various small roads, through the historic King Ranch. This 825,000-acre ranch is bigger than the state of Rhode Island. It is the largest working ranch in the United States and one of the oldest. From there I headed toward Rio Grande City along the Rio Grande, or the Rio Bravo as it is called by people in Mexico. Everywhere I looked I saw prickly pear. It was getting hotter now. I wondered how Cabeza de Vaca and the other men felt, walking under this brutal sun. They had made their escape, only to fall into the hands of yet another tribe of Indians. Did they ever feel as though all was hopeless? Did they think they would ever see Spain again?

Although I could not know for certain if I had walked along any single part of the path the four took, I was definitely following their route, according to the experts. In the *Relación*, Cabeza de Vaca refers to mountains and rivers and certain distances from the sea. And always he mentions the prickly pear: "During the entire time we ate the prickly pears we suffered thirst and to remedy this we drank the juice of the prickly pears."

All of this information taken together—the rivers, the mountains, the prickly pear—convinced me I was on the right path.

Cabeza de Vaca the Healer

Somewhere between Alice, Texas, and the Rio Grande, Cabeza de Vaca's story takes one of its strangest turns. While living among the Avavares, Cabeza de Vaca and his comrades healed the sick. As Spanish Catholics, the men invoked Christ, chanted, and made the sign of the cross over those who were ill. Along with these Christian rituals, they may have combined native remedies.

Cabeza de Vaca even claimed to have brought the dead back to life. "I found the Indian with eyes up turned, without pulse and with all the marks of lifelessness." Later that night, Cabeza de Vaca writes that Indians told him "the dead man whom I attended in their presence had resuscitated, rising from his bed, had walked about, eaten and talked to them."

Some have suggested the Spaniards used their "healing powers" primarily as a way to get safely through the many tribes they encountered on the long journey to Mexico City. But what exactly were these powers? How mystical? How real? And were the men only pretending to be healers so they would not be killed? Although I

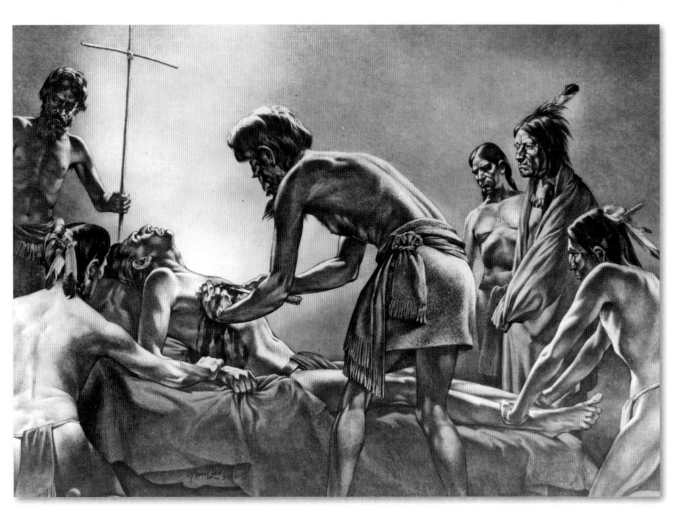

The First Recorded Surgical Operation in North America: Cabeza de Vaca, 1535, *painted by Texas artist Tom Lea.*

find this part of the story fascinating and difficult at times to imagine, Cabeza de Vaca reports that sick people were cured, and we have to take him at his word that he not only cured people as he passed through native lands, but he also believed totally in his own powers.

Cabeza de Vaca describes one of the first healings:

> Early the next day many Indians came and brought five people who were paralyzed and very ill, and they came for Castillo to cure them. Every one of the patients offered him his bow and arrows, which he accepted, and by sunset he made the sign of the cross over each of the sick, recommending them to God, Our Lord, and we all prayed to Him as well as we could to restore them to health. And He, seeing there was no other way of getting those people to help us so that we might be saved from our miserable existence, had mercy upon us, and in the morning all woke up well and hearty and went away in such good health as if they never had had any ailment whatever.

The Avavares celebrated and danced for three days. "[A]ll of us had to become medicine men. I was the most daring and reckless of all in undertaking cures. We never treated anyone that did not afterwards say he was well, and they had such confidence in our skill as to believe that none of them would die as long as we were among them."

Cabeza de Vaca the Surgeon

Later in his journey, somewhere beyond Monclova, Cabeza de Vaca the healer became a surgeon. An Indian was in great pain, an arrowhead lodged in his chest. Using his moderate knowledge of medicine, Cabeza de Vaca cut into the man with a knife and took out the flint. He sewed the incision shut with stitches and stopped the bleeding with a wad of shredded animal hide.

> So, with a knife, I cut open the breast as far as the place. The arrow point had gotten athwart, and was very difficult to remove. By cutting deeper, and inserting the point of the knife, with great difficulty I got it out; it was very long. Then, with a deer-bone, according to my knowledge of surgery, I made two stitches. After I had extracted the arrow they begged me for it, and I gave it to them. The whole village came back to look at it, and they sent it further inland that the people there might see it also. On account of this cure they made many dances and festivities, as is their custom. The next day I cut the stitches, and the Indian was well. The cut I had made only showed a scar like a line in the palm of the hand, and he said that he felt not the least pain.

The man recovered and Cabeza de Vaca was then, and continues to be, considered the first surgeon of the Southwest. Today the symbol of the Texas Surgical Society is the head of a cow imposed on the Star of Texas. It commemorates the first surgery in Texas performed by Cabeza de Vaca, whose name means "head of a cow."

From October 1534 to August 1535, the Spaniards and the Indians traveled together between the Nueces River and the Rio Grande. Although they suffered great hunger and ate nothing but roots, the men lived in complete freedom among the Avavares.

Finally, midsummer 1535, almost seven years after coming ashore in the Galveston area and after living among the friendly Avavares, Cabeza de Vaca and his three companions set off for Mexico City, the capital of New Spain. The prickly-pear fruit, the tuna, was just beginning to ripen.

Miracle Worker?

Did Cabeza de Vaca and his companions really heal the sick? Or did he exaggerate those claims in the book he presented to the king of Spain? It's one of the mysterious aspects of Cabeza de Vaca's adventure. Not only does he report that he cured many sick people on his journey, but he even says he brought one man back from the dead. Like traditional folk healers living in the Southwest, Cabeza de Vaca performed many of the same rituals as those of native medicine men, or curanderos (from the Spanish verb curar, *"to heal"). He was considered a folk saint by the people he encountered in the desert; he was a charismatic leader; and he believed he had received the gift of healing from God. Certainly the people he cured believed in him.*

In the next eight months, they would cover more than 2,500 miles and meet many Indian groups, crossing rivers and deserts on one of the great treks of all time.

Crossing the Rio Grande

If we assume that Cabeza de Vaca went south and west, he must have crossed the Rio Grande somewhere between Brownsville and Laredo. Dr. Chipman thinks it might have been around the city of Roma, Texas, which has been a crossing point on the Rio Grande for thousands of years.

As I drove up the Rio Grande from Roma, I smelled honey. The desert air was sweet with honey-mesquite blossoms, which looked like furry yellow caterpillars scattered over the thorny brush.

Now here was Falcon Lake, a large body of water formed when the Falcon Dam was built on the Rio Grande in 1953 for irrigation, power,

Many historians believe that somewhere in this vicinity Cabeza de Vaca crossed the Rio Grande.

Sixteenth-century Cabeza de Vaca might be amazed by the sight of the twenty-first-century Rio Grande, where it flows through Laredo.

flood control, and recreation. The actual trail of the survivors may very well lie beneath the lake.

This first crossing of the Rio Grande into what is Mexico today wasn't the end of Cabeza de Vaca's time in Texas. When he crossed the river, he turned north along a chain of mountains, and some days later he crossed the Rio Grande again, probably at Presidio, Texas, near the Rio Conchas. In all of Cabeza de Vaca's travels, he had never seen what he found here among the Jumano people—permanent settlements. Since there are other corroborating records of these permanent Indian settlements that existed around today's town of Presidio, we know that this is one of the few actual places on Cabeza de Vaca's direct route.

A Tantalizing Clue

Don and Marilynn Olson, professors at Texas State University at San Marcos, had traveled in 1996 with a group of professors and students by van to a remote canyon four hours south of

Honey-mesquite blossoms were another source of food for native people.

In Mexico, Don and Marilynn Olson (on the right), along with other professors and students, found evidence of Cabeza de Vaca's trail: nut-bearing pine trees.

the U.S. border near an industrial city called Monclova. They had driven on a washboard road along a dried-up riverbed to find a pine tree similar to the type yielding pine, or piñon, nuts that Cabeza de Vaca says he and his companions ate voraciously while traveling.

Chipman had said, "Olson's work is a critical piece validating the coastal route rather than the trans-Texas route because of the existence of these soft-shelled piñon nuts, which are found only in two areas. And they happen to be exactly where Cabeza de Vaca said they were, if you accept the coastal route."

I wanted to find those pine trees in Mexico that the Olsons had written about. So while at Texas State University to study the original manuscript of Cabeza de Vaca's *Relación*, I met Don and Marilynn in the Physics Department a few buildings away from the library. I was greeted by perhaps the most energetic man I've ever met.

Don Olson pulled out a photocopy of a page from the *Relación* and pointed to the passage about eating the pine nuts. He translated slowly:

"At nightfall we arrived at many houses that were located on the bank of a very beautiful river. And the owners of them came out halfway to welcome us, with their children on their backs. ... They ate the fruit of prickly pears and nuts from pine trees. In that land there are small pine trees and the cones of these are like small eggs, but the pine nuts are better than those of Castile, because they have very thin shells. ..."

Olson, who worked with botanists and geologists to evaluate the geographical evidence of Cabeza de Vaca's journey, had challenged the views of earlier writers who strongly stated their belief that he must have taken the northern route. One of the biggest believers in the trans-Texas theory was Cleve Hallenbeck. In 1940 he wrote an article in which he claimed that there were no nut-bearing pines in central Coahuila, Mexico, and therefore Cabeza de Vaca could not possibly have gone south.

The piñon nuts were found where Cabeza de Vaca said they were.

Don Olson traces what he believes was Cabeza de Vaca's southern route.

"But look at this," said Don as he unrolled some brightly colored geologic maps. He pinpointed a small canyon near Monclova in the state of Coahuila. It was in fact here that the Texas State group had traveled in 1996 to locate the piñon nuts from the papershell pine, or *pinus remota*.

"The canyon is called El Chilpitin," he said, leaning over his maps. "It is right here. We walked up these arroyos and found pines, the kinds of pines that Hallenbeck said did not exist in this part of Mexico."

With a mischievous smile, he pointed to two white coolers on the top shelf of a bookcase and said, "Those have not been opened in possibly ten years." But Olson wasn't about to open the coolers just yet.

First, he showed me copies of every map ever made on the route of Cabeza de Vaca. Then he brought out a prize possession—the map of Davenport and Wells. In 1919 historians Harbert Davenport and Joseph K. Wells offered the first serious interpretation proposing the "southern route," one that showed that the four survivors had journeyed south, not west or north, before heading into Mexico. The map was large and clear, and I studied it closely.

I told Olson I hoped to get to the canyon, and he said, "Good luck. It won't be easy." He generously photocopied many of his maps for me to take on my journey.

Before I departed, Don and Marilynn brought down the coolers from the upper shelf. Inside were boxes. Of course, I knew what was in them—the piñon nuts, pine boughs, and

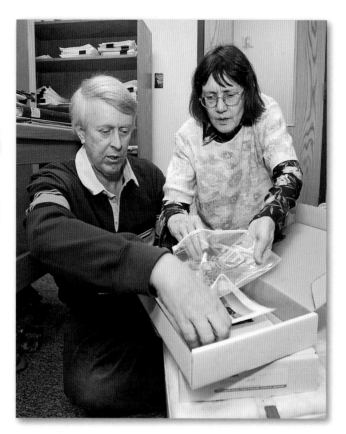

pinecones they had collected so many years ago.

Olson said, "When I open this, it'll smell like Christmas, just for a few seconds." With a grin, he ripped the lids off and we put our noses to the boxes, and for about five seconds it was indeed Christmas.

El Chilpitín

After Cabeza de Vaca first crossed the Rio Grande into what is Mexico today, he writes, "There we began to see mountains, and it seemed as if they swept down from the direction of the North Sea [Gulf of Mexico], and so, from what the Indians told us, we believe they are fifteen leagues from the ocean."

This passage is the one concrete reference that "southern route" interpreters of *The Account* refer to when they point to Cabeza de Vaca's turning inland. The chain of mountains, or *sierra* as he calls

I eagerly waited for Don and Marilynn Olson to open the boxes from the coolers.

In 1919 historians Harbert Davenport and Joseph K. Wells created a map showing the various routes taken by Cabeza de Vaca.

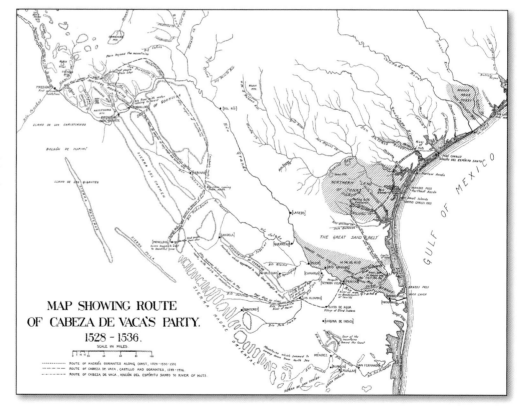

MAP SHOWING ROUTE OF CABEZA DE VACA'S PARTY. 1528 - 1536.

Cabeza de Vaca mentions these mountains in his account, which led me to believe that I was still on the trail.

it, was about forty-five miles from the Gulf and probably refers to the Sierra Madre near Monclova.

In Laredo, Texas, Juan Manuel Zambrano Gonzalez helped me with the final stretch of my journey. At 4:00 a.m., we climbed into his four-wheel vehicle and headed over the border and down to Monclova to look for Olson's canyon. In El Chilpitin, I would not only see evidence that the survivors had taken the southern route home, but I would also come as close as I ever could to walking in the footsteps of Cabeza de Vaca.

As it grew light over the desert, I saw we were in a vast, flat country, filled with prickly pear. In the air was the scent of honey mesquite. The far-off chain of dark, ragged-toothed mountains was like a distant smudge against the sky. When we reached Monclova, Juan spotted a pickup with a decal of a deer on the back. He knew it belonged to a hunter, and hunters know their canyons, he said. I couldn't believe our luck. The hunter said, indeed, he knew the way to the canyon and pointed us in the right direction. We followed

the pickup on a dirt road leading out of town, then headed off by ourselves. After ten miles down the deserted, dusty road, we realized we were running

Juan Zambrano tries to find the way into the canyon.

Was Cabeza de Vaca here?

parallel to the mountains. We could see a gash in the sierras, and surely that had to be El Chilpitin. But how could we get there?

We came across an old man on a buggy and another in a pickup truck. The men knew El Chilpitin, but disagreed on how to reach it. Each gave us completely different directions. The men drove off, leaving us in the dust and no closer to the canyon. Finally, after a number of wrong turns, we managed to find the way.

Up ahead was El Chilpitin. The only thing between us and the canyon now was a metal gate. We pulled it open and entered the canyon silently, as if we had reached some sacred ruin.

The canyon was littered with car-sized boulders along a wide, dried-up riverbed. Juan said that when the rains arrive in May, it would become a raging river.

The first "pine" we found looked like the right shape—twenty-five feet tall, its branches bunched like the papershell pine I'd seen in photographs that Olson had showed me. Even though there were no nuts on the ground and no smell of Christmas trees, I was convinced it was a papershell pine. We found it!

We left the car and made our way slowly up the rugged canyon. We found a few dead trees, too, which I thought might be the same pines Olson had found. They looked like dead versions of the pine trees in his photographs. Maybe this drought has killed them, Juan said. And this indeed seemed like the exact spot where Olson and his group had stood for a photograph—or so I thought.

I was thrilled that we'd found the remote canyon, and even more excited about the remote pines, dead or not. I knew, of course, that the presence of these pines did not prove that the four men had come to this exact canyon, but rather that they had passed somewhere near here on their way north to Presidio and then west to the Pacific coast of Mexico. It did prove, however, that there were indeed nut-bearing pine trees in central Coahuila, Mexico.

After inspecting the fourth "pine," we headed back to the truck elated. Riding out of the canyon, I cast my eyes backward, but the trees were already hidden by the rim of the canyon walls.

I slapped Juan on the back. We cheered. We had found the canyon and I had found my historical gold—the gold of pine trees.

But it was fool's gold.

Later, I saw my mistake. I'd brought back a few boughs of my "pine tree." In my hotel room, I sniffed the boughs, but there was not a trace of Christmas in them. The trees were not pine at all. They were probably salt cedar, a botanist told me later. If there were any pines left, they must have been hidden farther up the canyon, and I'd missed them by not driving deeper into El Chilpitin. No wonder there were no cones or nuts beneath those trees.

I was like the conquistadors blinded by their desire to find gold. I had seen what I wanted to see. In my desire for historical discovery, I had made pine trees out of cedars.

Setting out on the Texas trail of Cabeza de Vaca, perhaps I'd been chasing ghosts. I wasn't sure what I'd find. But after weeks of travel in the Lone Star State and Mexico, I feel certain I had touched upon his trail many times. At the very least, I'd seen firsthand that stark and haunting terrain the conquistador had braved nearly five centuries ago.

Up ahead, El Chilpitin canyon.

And, in testimony of, that what I have stated in the foregoing narrative is true, I hereunto sign my name—

A Different Kind of Conquistador

The jagged ranges of the great Sierra Madre that run north-south through Mexico blocked Cabeza de Vaca from moving easily to the west. Instead of walking south from the Monclova area, he and his companions moved north, then west through the Mexican desert to the Pacific Ocean. He had thought the ocean would be much closer than it actually was. The survivors followed an ancient trail that had been used for trade between the Pueblo people in the north and the peoples of Central America to the south. All along the trail, native people received the men as great healers.

They were the first Europeans to cross Mexico to the Pacific. When they reached the ocean, they walked south hundreds and hundreds of miles and began to see signs that Spaniards had been there. Many of the native people they met feared Cabeza de Vaca and the other men because Spaniards had ridden through these areas in search of slaves. The slavers "had destroyed and burnt the villages, taking with them half of the men and all the women and children." Despite these atrocities, Cabeza de Vaca and his companions were able to make friends with the people.

Cabeza de Vaca and Esteban were out ahead of Dorantes and Castillo by maybe thirty miles, traveling with a group of eleven Indians in late January or early February 1536, when they suddenly came upon the Spanish slavers, the first Europeans other than themselves that they had seen in years. Cabeza de Vaca and Esteban were sunbaked and nearly naked.

Cabeza de Vaca writes:

The next morning I came upon four Christians on horseback, who, seeing me in such a strange attire, and in company with Indians, were greatly startled. They stared at me for quite a while, speechless; so great was their surprise that they could not find words to ask me anything. I spoke first, and told them to lead me to their captain, and we went together to Diego de Alcaraza, their commander.

What a strange meeting this must have been. Cabeza de Vaca announced to the slavers that he and his three fellow travelers were survivors of a shipwreck that had occurred eight years before and thousands of miles away. To locate the other two survivors miles behind, Alcaraza "at once dispatched three horsemen, with fifty of his Indians, and the negro went with them as guide, while I remained and asked them to give me a certified statement of the date, year, month, and day when I had met them, also the condition in which I had come, with which request they complied."

Diego de Alcaraza and his men wanted to take the Indians who traveled with the survivors as slaves. But Cabeza de Vaca would not allow it. "Thereupon we had many and bitter quarrels with the Christians, for they wanted to make slaves of our Indians, and we grew so angry at it."

Many months later, on July 23, 1536, Cabeza de Vaca and his companions finally reached Mexico City.

The final leg of their journey had taken them up the Texas side of the Rio Grande, where they had crossed back into Mexico somewhere around Lajitas, Texas. From that point onward, they had made one of the great journeys of all time. They had traveled all the way to the Pacific Ocean, which took seven months. Then they marched down the Pacific coast and inland until they reached the former Aztec capital. No one could believe they were still alive.

The sudden appearance of Cabeza de Vaca and his three companions in Mexico City in 1536 fueled more speculation about the mysterious land to the north. The Spaniards heard the survivors tell extraordinary stories of their adventures. They talked about the different groups of people they had met and the settlements and cultivated lands they had seen. They also told stories about the fabled Seven Cities of Gold, which made the Spaniards even thirstier for treasure.

Did the survivors really believe such wonders existed? Or did they embroider the truth at times? All we know is that their stories must have been powerful, for it was their accounts that sparked a new wave of explorations and adventures—and atrocities. Soon, Juan de Oñate and Coronado and de Soto, among other conquistadors, struck out from New Spain seeking riches. They marched up the Rio Grande and into what is now New Mexico, Arizona, and Kansas. As a consequence, many native peoples would suffer from the conquistadors' thirst for treasure and land.

In 1540 Coronado led an expedition in search of the Seven Cities of Gold (Coronado's March–Colorado by Frederic Remington, 1897).

The Seven Cities of Gold

According to an old legend, seven bishops fled Spain after the invasion of the Moors in the eighth century, and each founded a wealthy city on an island somewhere in the Atlantic Ocean. When Spanish explorers failed to find the island, they thought the seven cities must be in the New World. Tales of great cities—massive buildings covered with precious gems—that lay somewhere north of Mexico fueled the legend. Some historians believe that a pueblo, possibly the Pueblo of Zuni, with its tall buildings and walls decorated with turquoise, was mistaken for one of the Seven Cities of Gold.

Based on these stories, Antonio de Mendoza, the viceroy, or governor, of New Spain, launched a scouting expedition. When the men returned, they brought new stories of the Seven Cities. Powerful tales like these inflamed the hearts of other conquistadors such as Coronado and Hernando de Alvarado, who headed north on

The Pueblo of Zuni, in a photograph taken between 1879 and 1881. Could conquistadors have mistaken this for one of the Seven Cities of Gold?

their own expeditions in search of the Seven Cities of Gold. Somewhere on the plains of Texas, one native captive told Alvarado a story about a great realm called Quivira.

Quivira and Cíbola were two of the fabled seven cities. The conquistadors must have thought they were close to finding something. Esteban, who survived his long ordeal in the wilderness, later served as a scout on an expedition to the north, only to lose his life in the quest. From 1540 to 1542, the conquistadors furiously crisscrossed what is now the southwestern United States in their hunt for riches—all in vain.

A Changed Man

Cabeza de Vaca spent eight months in Mexico City before he embarked on a four-month sea journey back to Spain. By this time, Cabeza de Vaca had gained great personal power. He could walk a whole day without food. He and his companions had grown tough. They were no longer the people they had been when they left Spain for the region called La Florida.

While other conquistadors hoped to find gold, Cabeza de Vaca found something more. He underwent a transformation during his long ordeal. He had lived among the native peoples. He had been comforted, fed, mistreated, enslaved, and embraced by many. Maybe he had learned something other conquistadors had not. He came to see the people of the New World not as savages, as did many conquistadors, but as human beings like himself, with a capacity for love and hate, good and evil. What greater gold could be found than this truth?

Perhaps in the end it doesn't matter where exactly he traveled, though it is great fun and exciting to speculate about such a historical event. One thing is for sure, though: Álvar Núñez Cabeza de Vaca, the first European Texan, had experienced one of the greatest adventures of all time—and survived to tell the tale.

Map of the New World

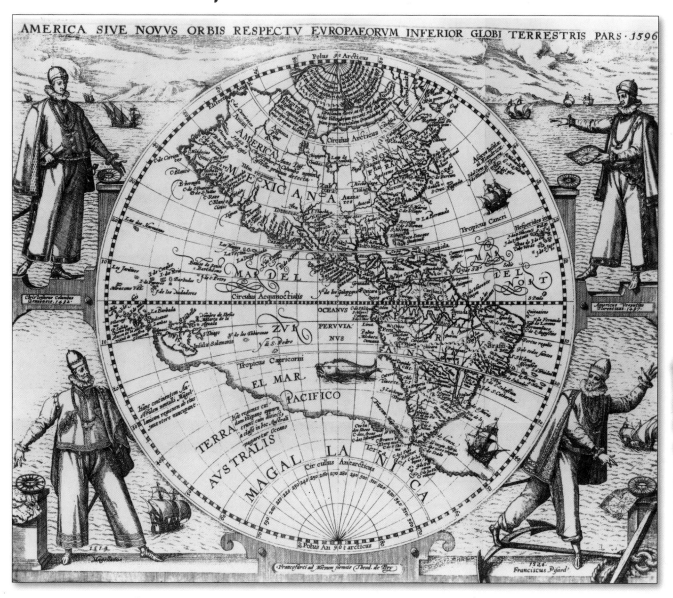

AMERICA SIVE NOVVS ORBIS RESPECTV EVROPAEORVM INFERIOR GLOBI TERRESTRIS PARS · 1596

This 1596 map of the New World, featuring (clockwise from top left) Columbus, Vespucci, Pizarro, and Magellan, was made almost forty years after the death of Cabeza de Vaca. Created in Frankfurt, Germany, by cartographer Theodore de Bray, the map incorporates information acquired by sixteenth-century explorers during what is known as the Age of Discovery.

Timeline

Conquest and Exploration

1492: Searching for a sea route to India, Christopher Columbus makes landfall on an island in the Bahamas archipelago. He names the island San Salvador.

1500: Pedro Álvars Cabral reaches Brazil and claims it for Portugal.

1509: Ponce de León founds the first settlement in Puerto Rico, and as governor he helps enslave the Taíno, the island's native people.

1513: Vasco Núñez de Balboa discovers the Pacific Ocean.

1514: Spanish colonies established in Panama.

1519–1521: Hernán Cortés leads an expedition to conquer the Aztec Empire.

1519–1522: Ferdinand Magellan of Portugal circumnavigates the globe. He dies before the journey ends.

1528–1536: Cabeza de Vaca travels from present-day Florida, through Texas, and across northern Mexico.

1532–1533: Francisco Pizarro leads an expedition to conquer the Inca Empire.

1536: Cabeza de Vaca and the surviving members of his expedition reach Mexico City.

1540: Hernando de Soto finds and crosses the Mississippi River.

1540–1542: Francisco Vásquez de Coronado explores much of what is now the southwestern United States.

1541–1542: Francisco de Orellana follows the Amazon River across South America to the Atlantic Ocean.

Notable Conquistadors

Vasco Núñez de Balboa (1475–1519) sailed to the New World after hearing of the voyages of Christopher Columbus. In 1513, searching for a kingdom rich in gold, he crossed the Isthmus of Panama and reached the Pacific Ocean. He claimed it and all the coastal lands for Spain.

Francisco Pizarro (c. 1471–1541) captured the Inca ruler Atahualpa (ah-tah-WALL-pah) at Cajamarca in what is known as the Siege of the Incas. Pizarro demanded a ransom for the king's release: a room filled with vast quantities of gold and silver. The Incas delivered the ransom. Nevertheless, Pizarro executed Atahualpa and went on to conquer the Inca Empire.

Francisco Vásquez de Coronado (c. 1510–1554) led an expedition into what is now the southwestern United States and Texas in search of the Seven Cities of Gold. Soldiers from his expedition were the first Europeans to see the Grand Canyon.

Juan Ponce de León (c. 1460–1521) sailed with Christopher Columbus on his second voyage. Later, he became governor of Puerto Rico. He is associated with the legend of the Fountain of Youth, but it was actually his search for riches that brought him to the shores of Florida.

Hernando de Soto (c. 1496–1542) served under Francisco Pizarro during the conquest of the Inca Empire. Later, he organized an expedition to Florida in search of gold. He explored much of what is now the southeastern United States and crossed the Mississippi River to explore what is now known as Arkansas, Oklahoma, and Texas.

Hernán Cortés (1485–1547) marched on Mexico with an army of about six hundred soldiers. He conquered the Aztec Empire and destroyed its capital. On its ruins, he built Mexico City.

Bibliography

(All Web sites active at time of publication)

Books for Adults

Barr, Alwyn. *The African Texans*. College Station: Texas A&M University Press, 2004.

———. *Black Texans: A History of African Americans in Texas, 1528–1995*. Norman: University of Oklahoma Press, 1996.

Cabeza de Vaca, Álvar Núñez. *The Journey of Álvar Núñez Cabeza de Vaca, Translated from His Own Narrative* by Fanny Bandelier. Edited with an introduction by Adolph F. Bandelier. New York: A. S. Barnes, 1905.

———. *The Narrative of Cabeza de Vaca*. Edited and translated by Rolena Adorno and Patrick Charles Pautz. Lincoln: University of Nebraska Press, 2003.

Cox, Paul W., and Patty Leslie. *Texas Trees: A Friendly Guide*. San Antonio: Corona Publishing, 1999.

Hallenbeck, Cleve. *Álvar Núñez Cabeza de Vaca: The Journey and Route of the First European to Cross the Continent of North America, 1534–1536*. Glendale, CA: Arthur H. Clark, 1940.

Krieger, Alex D. *We Came Naked and Barefoot: The Journey of Cabeza de Vaca across North America*. Texas Archaeology and Ethnohistory Series. Austin: University of Texas Press, 2002.

La Vere, David. *The Texas Indians*. College Station: Texas A&M University Press, 2004.

Schneider, Paul. *Brutal Journey: The Epic Story of the First Crossing of North America*. New York: Henry Holt, 2006.

Wood, Michael. *Conquistadors*. Berkeley: University of California Press, 2000.

Articles

Chipman, Donald E. "In Search of Cabeza de Vaca's Route across Texas: A Historiographical Survey." *Southwestern Historical Quarterly* 91 (October 1987): 127–48.

Davenport, Harbert, and Joseph K. Wells. "The First Europeans in Texas, 1528–1536." Pts. 1 and 2. *Southwestern Historical Quarterly* (October 1918): 111–42; (January 1919): 205–59. (Available online at Southwestern Historical Quarterly Online: www.tsha.utexas.edu/publications/journals/shq/online/v022/n2/contrib_DIVL1362.html)

Text Online

PBS: New Perspectives on the West. www.pbs.org/weta/thewest/resources/archives/one/cabeza.htm (online text of *The Journey of Álvar Núñez Cabeza de Vaca*, translated by Fanny Bandelier).

Books for Young Readers

Childress, Diana. *Barefoot Conquistador: Cabeza de Vaca and the Struggle for Native American Rights*. Minneapolis: Twenty-first Century Books, 2008.

Johnston, Lissa Jones. *Crossing a Continent: The Incredible Journey of Cabeza de Vaca*. Austin, TX: Eakin Press, 1997.

Marrin, Albert. *Empires Lost and Won: The Spanish Heritage in the Southwest*. New York: Atheneum, 1997.

Menard, Valerie. *Álvar Núñez Cabeza de Vaca*. Bear, DE: Mitchell Lane Publishers, 2003.

Waldman, Stuart. *We Asked for Nothing: The Remarkable Journey of Cabeza de Vaca*. New York: Mikaya Press, 2003.

Web Sites

Center for the Study of the Southwest, Texas State University. Windows to the Unknown: Cabeza de Vaca's Journey to the Southwest. swrhc.txstate.edu/cssw/resources/cdvwindows/index.php

Lehigh University. *Cabeza de Vaca* (film, 1991). www.lehigh.edu/~ineng/pag2/pag2-title.html

PBS: Conquistadors. www.pbs.org/conquistadors/

Texas Council for the Humanities Resource Center. Cabeza de Vaca's American Journey. www.humanities-interactive.org/crossroads/game/game.html

Texas Indians. www.texasindians.com

Texas State Historical Association. www.tshaonline.org

Index

Page numbers in *italics* refer to images